Where the Wild Goose Flies

Contents

Introduction.......................................2

Winter...4

Spring...12

Summer..21

Autumn..28

Glossary..29

Facts about the Pink-footed Goose... 30

Index...32

Introduction

There are eight different kinds of wild geese that spend part of their time in Britain.

This book is about one kind, the Pink-footed Goose. It describes the life of one goose and her family. The goose that this book will follow is a female called **MOM**. She is called that because those are the letters on a white plastic ring that an **ornithologist** put on her right leg. On her left leg is a metal ring with the number 4073412 on it. Her mate has only a metal ring, with the number 4138640 on it.

Pink-footed Goose

The eight different kinds of wild geese drawn to scale.

Greylag Goose

Brent Goose

Barnacle Goose

Lesser White-fronted Goose

White-fronted Goose

Canada Goose

Bean Goose

Ringing

Some geese and other sorts of birds carry metal rings on their legs. Each one has a number that is different from all of the others. As the birds fly from one part of the world to another, they are trapped in a way that does not harm them. They are then ringed by ornithologists. The rings do not hurt the birds at all. One goose has worn its ring for over twenty years. The rings help the scientists to discover many things about the way that the birds live and the journeys that they make.

A few birds also have plastic rings with big letters on them, like MOM's. The letters show up clearly and on a bright day a scientist with a telescope can recognize individual birds from a distance of as much as 275 metres. Birds that wear this sort of ring can be followed and studied much more easily. Big rings can tell us lots of details about how birds live. For example, one pair of Pink-footed Geese, both of which have white rings, always come back to the same part of a particular golf course in Lancashire early each winter. It is likely that others have similar spots to return to.

Winter

January 1st

Exactly as the clock struck midnight, the bells of the church in the little Norfolk village began to chime. They were ringing in the New Year. The sound floated across the flat, frosty countryside. Three kilometres away, MOM stirred in her sleep, roused by the unusual noise. She raised her head from where it had been tucked warmly under her **scapular feathers**. All around her, geese were waking and calling, their bright eyes shining in the moonlight.

They were not seriously frightened, for they were used to the strange noises made by people. They took no notice of the rumble of traffic or the growl of aircraft. Even the lights of cars and lorries at night did not trouble them. They had nothing to fear in their safe roosting place, which was on the water that covered the salt marshes at high tide. Soon the whole flock was asleep again. They bobbed on the wavelets whipped up by the same wind that carried the sound of bells.

The year really began for MOM when the first gleam of dawn streaked the sky with pink. She woke suddenly, half stood up in the shallow water, ducked her head and stretched her wings. Then she waggled her tail vigorously from side to side. The ripples roused her mate. His movements woke the two members of their family that had slept close by. Other nearby birds were disturbed and soon 200 geese were stretching, splashing water over themselves and calling to each other.

MOM's mate suddenly began to shake his head from side to side. Other members of the family did the same. Without making a sound, they were giving a message that could be understood by other geese. Twenty birds that had slept near to each other sprang into the air. With strong wingbeats they rose quickly above the water. They did not fly far. On a farm on the outskirts of a village about 12 kilometres away, sugar beet had been harvested and the leafy tops left on the field. When they reached it, the geese circled. They did not come to the ground until they were sure that there was nothing unusual about. Though the field was large, they landed in a bunch. The **gaggle** stayed close together as they worked their way along, always keeping a sharp lookout in case of danger. They had no need to worry on the sugar beet, but other fields in the area had been sown with winter barley. There the feeding birds damaged the growing plants. The farmer tried to protect his crop with bird scarers that flapped in the wind and twice a day somebody walked round the barley fields. This was enough to frighten the geese back to places where they would do no harm and where they would be left undisturbed to feed all day.

A **skein** of Pink-footed Geese

Pink-footed Geese grazing in a field

January *5th*

In the night, a northerly gale blew up, bringing frozen snow hissing along the surface of the water where MOM and her family were roosting. Their oily outer feathers kept them perfectly dry and a thick layer of **down** close to their skin prevented them from getting cold.

Later in the day the wind ruffled their feathers as they grazed, making them uneasy. Early in the afternoon MOM and her family and about 150 other geese left the field. They did not head for their usual **roost**, but turned north-west, flying inland. They flew high, in small groups. They travelled in an arrowhead formation, with one of the older birds in the lead. They called to each other as they flew. Few people heard their yelping cries as they made their way over the great cities of the Midlands, where the noise of the traffic drowned out almost all other sounds.

Pink-footed Geese flying in arrowhead formation

Lancashire

The Wash

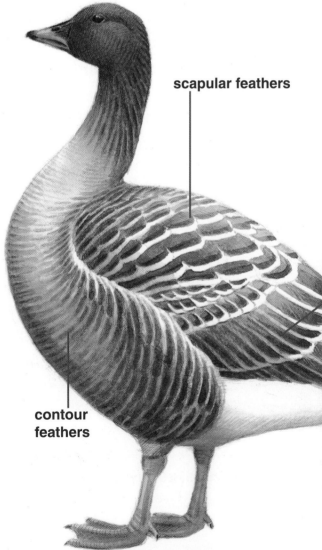

scapular feathers

contour feathers

6

January 5th

Early in the morning, at The Wildfowl & Wetlands Trust's **reserve** at Martin Mere in Lancashire, one of the wardens was looking across the marshy fields. Suddenly he realized that birds that had not been there before were feeding in the pasture. He could see that one of them was wearing a big white ring. Through his binoculars he could read the letters MOM. Later that day, as he filled in the log book, he checked up on MOM. She had been ringed at Martin Mere seven years ago and had been back every year since then. She had been luckier than some of the geese, which had disappeared. A few had been shot by wildfowlers, one had been hit by lightning in a thunderstorm, and some had just not been seen again. Perhaps they had visited the reserve, but nobody had noticed them.

flight feathers

tail feathers

For several weeks MOM and her family stayed near to Martin Mere. Sometimes they fed on the reserve fields. On other days they travelled to fields where **stubble** had not been ploughed back into the earth. They could still find grain there. One of the best places was a field where potatoes had been grown. The farmer had harvested all the big potatoes, but there were still lots of tiny ones in the ground. These were good food for geese, and for once, the farmer did not feel cross at seeing them. They were not taking food that he wanted for crops, but cleaning the field and at the same time enriching the soil with their droppings.

February *12th*

Though she did not know it, changes were beginning to take place inside MOM's body. She would soon be able to lay eggs because of these changes. For the time being, the only change that could be seen was that she was more restless than her mate. She often stood and pointed her head towards the north. On February 12th, many of the geese left Martin Mere. They flew towards Scotland, along the backbone of England, over the Southern Uplands and the Firth of Forth.

Scotland

Lancashire

The lights of Edinburgh meant nothing to the geese. Soon after they had left the city behind, they pitched down by a great **loch**. Here were green fields with small ponds, just right for geese. The place where they landed is called Vane Farm. This is a famous reserve owned by the Royal Society for the Protection of Birds, where many water birds find safe places to feed and roost.

Whooper swans on Loch Leven near Vane Farm.

An aerial view of Vane Farm

9

Lots of people saw MOM while she was at Vane Farm. Some watched from the **hide** set up for visitors and school parties. Other watched through very big binoculars. MOM's white ring was soon singled out and several children did projects about MOM and her family.

Spring

As the spring days grew longer and the grass grew sweeter, the geese moved further north. They fed hard and grew fatter. Birdwatchers could see that their undersides looked swollen. This was fat that would be needed for fuel on the journey that they would soon make.

What Pink-footed Geese eat

Type of food	often eaten	not often eaten
cereal grains	✔	
growing cereals		✔
grass	✔	
roots and tubers	✔	

April *21st*

The flock had been in northern Scotland for several days. MOM had fed with the others, but like most of the females in the flock, she often pointed still further north. The night of the 21st was clear, with brilliant stars and a slight wind from the south. That evening, instead of returning to their roost, the geese rose higher and higher into the air. Eventually, they were 1000 metres above the ground. Then the arrowhead flights swung to a north-westerly direction, and flew from the land.

Still climbing, they left behind the dim shapes and lights of the Hebrides and were soon flying over some of the wildest seas in the world. They levelled out at a height of about 4000 metres. They were flying fast, at about 60 kilometres per hour. Like a person running, they became very hot. The temperature of the air at this height was well below freezing, but to the geese this was a bonus because it helped them to keep cool.

Nobody understands how geese know in which direction to fly. We know that they navigate by the stars, but how they do it is still a mystery to us. An old bird, which had made the journey many times before, led the **skein**. Sometimes it was MOM, sometimes one of the others took over, for the leading bird has the most tiring flight. Behind the leader, the others flew in steady diagonal lines. Each bird watched and kept its distance from the white rump of the one ahead. Below them they saw the occasional twinkle of lights from a big fishing boat. Above them they heard the drone of planes making a **great circle flight** between Europe and America. The geese took no notice of the boats or the planes and flew on unwaveringly through the night and the next day.

April *22nd*

About one o'clock in the afternoon, the geese saw a shadow on the horizon. It was the distant outline of Iceland. Now that their target was in sight, they flew lower, until by late afternoon they were only a few metres above the waves. They landed before dark, and roosted that night 1100 kilometres from the place where they had last slept.

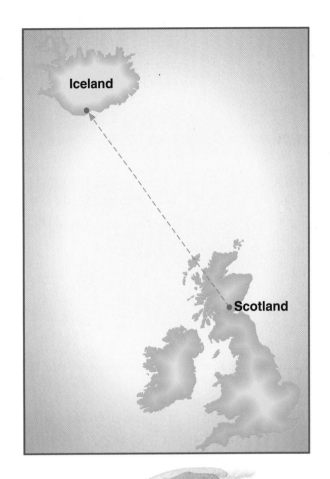

April *23rd* —May *14th*

After their long journey, MOM and the other geese were hungry. They had used up the fat that their bodies had built up before they left Scotland. Now they had to feed as hard as they could. There was still some deep snow in southern Iceland, but round the edges of some of the hayfields a rim of green was showing. The geese flocked to these places, gobbling the tender growing shoots.

The south-west of Iceland

15

Each day more and more geese arrived, until about 20 000 birds were following the retreating snow, feeding on the new grass. The males fed less than their mates. They spent a great deal of time standing near to the females, as if guarding them. It is lucky for the farmers of southern Iceland that the geese do not stay long in their fields, or they would never be able to harvest any hay. After about three weeks the Pink-footed Geese left and flew north once more. Many of them, including MOM and her mate, went to an area in the centre of the country. This place is like an island. It is not surrounded by water, but by a cold, stony region. Very few enemies of the geese could cross this place. If they did, they would find little hills of stone and sand, called moraines. Moraines were formed by ancient glaciers thousands of years ago. Today, the moraines give shelter from bad weather and make a safe nesting place for the geese.

MOM and her mate arrived at their final destination. It was near the top of a sandy ridge, where they had nested in earlier years. Small streams ran down the slope, forming boggy pools on the flatter ground.

May *16th*

MOM found the remains of the last year's nest. It was just a mound of grass and rushes on the ground. It still contained some old eggshells. She ate these up quickly, even though she was now fat. Eggshells contain **calcium** and she needed all the calcium that she could get to help her make new eggs. She settled on the old nest and moved round a bit to mould it to her shape. It was just big enough for her to sit in, and about 10 centimetres deep. She began to refurbish it with a few more bits of grass. Then she preened some of the soft down from her underside to make a warm mattress for her eggs. While she was doing this, her mate stood nearby, alert for any enemies.

During the next few days, 4138640 courted MOM. He drove away all other birds (and some imaginary enemies as well) and bowed in front of her. She replied by lowering her head. They called and stretched their wings. They dipped and shook their heads as they swam side by side in the pools and it was here that they mated.

Driving away other birds

Bowing and lowering heads

Swimming side by side

Mating

May 26th

Early in the day, MOM laid her first egg. It was white, and nearly twice as big as a hen's egg. As soon as it was laid, MOM covered it with more down from her body. Then she left it because she needed to feed.

For the next three days, she laid another egg each morning. By the time the last one was laid, the nest was full of down, tucked between and under the eggs. It did not hurt her to take so much, even though she was left with a bare patch on her underside. The bare patch helped her, for the heat of her body passed easily through her skin and warmed the eggs.

For the next three weeks MOM only left the nest for a few minutes each morning and evening, so that she could feed and drink. For much of the time she sat quite still, her brown back blending with the colours of her surroundings. Sometimes she stood up. She looked as if she were counting the eggs but usually she was turning them over, so that they should be warmed right through. In the early days she put more down over them, but soon the bare patch began to grow new feathers, and she could not pull these out.

MOM kept the eggs warm without any help from her mate. He stood guard, ready to protect her and the nest. For most of the time he was never more than five metres away. The main danger came from the sky. Flesh-eating birds, such as Snowy Owls and Arctic Skuas sometimes drifted over as they searched for food. If MOM had ever left the nest for long, a hungry gull would have swooped down to grab an egg. If they saw any of these predators, MOM and her mate would stretch their necks and call, to show that they were ready to defend themselves. One day, an Arctic Fox trotted along the ridge. Both of the geese were instantly alert. Instead of running away, the gander puffed up his feathers to make himself look bigger and half spread his wings. He stretched his neck and hissed. He looked and sounded so frightening that the fox came no closer, but went on his way to look for easier prey.

Summer

As MOM sat, the countryside changed round her. At first there were still patches of snow, but by early June the bright summer colours of the **tundra** were beginning to show themselves. The greens and golds of the leaves of many plants contrasted with the purple flowers of the cranesbill and the yellow flowers of the roseroot. In the south, the great shape of Heckla, Iceland's biggest volcano, could be seen, clear and cloudless. There was hardly any night, only a heavy twilight before the sun showed itself once more.

June 23rd

MOM looked asleep as she sat, but suddenly she was awake and alert. The eggs, which had been still and quiet for so long, showed the first signs of life. From one of them, MOM could hear a tiny clicking sound. She moved and bent her head to listen more closely, and then answered with a gentle cooing, quite different from her normal voice. Later in the day, she heard sounds from two more of the eggs.

June 25th

Calling came from the last egg on this day. The sound from the eggs was very faint, and so was MOM's reply. For nearly two days the chicks, though they were still safe inside the eggs, were aware of each others' and their mother's voices.

June *26th*

About the middle of the morning MOM heard a new sound. One of the chicks had begun to break its way through the eggshell. First a tiny hole appeared. Then slowly, a crack seemed to grow round the centre of the egg. With a great push from inside, the shell broke into two pieces. At last a **chick**, damp and exhausted with its efforts, lay in the nest.

Over the next few hours, the other three eggs hatched. For the first day of their lives the chicks stayed in the nest, and their downy feathers dried in the warmth of their mother's body. They needed to rest. Hatching is one of the most tiring things that a bird does in its whole life.

June *27th*

Mom and her mate and their new family left the nest. The chicks were rested and were hungry and ready to feed. Now both parents were on the look out for enemies. Snowy owls had chicks of their own that were crying for food and a **gosling** would have made a snack for them. All round them, other geese and their babies were moving away from their nests. The goslings made little cheeping noises. Their parents kept their **broods** close to them with soft answering calls. They stretched their necks and hissed if any other birds came too close to them. A high pitched yell from the parents meant danger, and the chicks came scuttling back to safety.

Snowy Owl

July *12th*

Flightless geese skimming the water of a lake in Iceland.

MOM's brood were growing fast. By now, each one weighed almost a kilogram, nearly half as much as she did. They still needed to be watched, but they wandered further from the adults, often joining other young ones and their parents.

Now that the main stress of caring for the very young chicks was over, the adults began to lose their feathers. All birds do this, but most keep enough feathers to fly. Geese and their close relatives the ducks and the swans are quite different. They lose all of the **flight feathers** on their wings at the same time, so they cannot fly at all. New feathers start to grow almost as soon as the old ones fall out, and in just over three weeks, the geese are airborne once more.

MOM lost her first flight feathers on July 12th. After this she and her family walked many kilometres each day, feeding on the low growing tundra plants. In the past, people used to round up geese when they were in this flightless stage, and kill them for winter food. The big flocks grazed their way past several low stone buildings, like huts without a roof. They did not realize that these were the places where the geese used to be herded and killed.

July *22nd*

A group of scientists had been watching the geese for a few days. Now the scientists appeared on the top of a low hill. The birds were not alarmed but they moved away, towards a small lake. The men and women walked after them. When the flock reached the edge of the water, where they would usually find safety, the people jumped into little boats and still followed them. Now the geese were a bit worried. They jostled closer and closer, calling to each other but unable to fly. The boats were behind them and on either side of them. They dared not go back, they could only go forwards on to the land on the other side. The first geese hurried up the slope, but now there was no escape. Nets, difficult to see from a distance, blocked their way. The birds behind pressed forward. The birds in the lead could not turn round. More people appeared, driving the geese on. Finally almost the whole flock was enclosed.

MOM and her family were some of the first birds into the nets. MOM was picked up by strong hands, and held so that she could not strike with her wings or beak. She was silent, as the ornithologist said, "MOM. UK 4073412". His partner wrote the number down in a big book. Then, the ornithologist smoothed MOM's feathers and popped her into a small netted **corral**.

When the scientists picked up a young bird, they put a metal ring on its right leg. Each ring had the address of the museum in **Reykjavik** and a seven figure number on it. Perhaps some time in the future somebody would find those birds. They would know that they were ringed in Iceland and would be able to find out their age and something of their movements. In the corral, the birds were quiet. Soon, the corral was opened and the geese rushed out, calling loudly. If each bird had been released as it was examined or ringed, it is likely that many of the goslings would have got lost. As it was, MOM found her family quite quickly, for among all the calling, each pair of parents recognised their own young. The geese hurried away from the place. The humans gathered up their nets, tired but pleased that they had caught and ringed almost the whole flock of over 200 geese.

August *1st*

MOM's family were growing and changing. They had lost their gosling down, and their bodies were now covered with feathers, though they were not yet able to fly. They still fed near to their parents, but neither of the adults drove other birds away as they did when the chicks were small. All their care had not prevented one of the chicks being snatched by a Snowy Owl, but three had survived.

August *21st*

The goslings were now as big and heavy as their parents. When they preened, or splashed in water they spread and flapped their wings. As they walked or ran, they sometimes stretched a wing to balance themselves. All of this helped to strengthen their flying muscles. Eight weeks after they had hatched, the goslings made their first short flight. After that, they flew every day, becoming stronger and more confident in the air. By now, the days were becoming shorter and colder and the first drifts of snow could be seen on the tops of the mountains. The males in the flock seemed to be anxious to leave but the females, like MOM, were too busy feeding to notice the way their mates were stretching their necks and pointing southwards.

Autumn

Iceland in the snow

September *16th*

MOM and her family had all their new feathers, glossy and strong. They were fat with rich food. The days were shortening and the time for feeding was getting less. The snow drifts were creeping down the mountain sides. On the night of September 16th, a cold wind blew from the north. Instead of going to their usual roost on a lake, MOM and her family swept into the air and away southwards. They flew high and fast, helped by the following wind, and by early next day they could see the hills of Scotland in the distance. Nobody saw their first landing place, but they moved the next day to stubble fields where they could rest and feed and begin to gain strength for the coming winter.

September *23rd*

The warden at Martin Mere made a note in the log book that an old friend had returned safely. He saw MOM and her mate and three young birds feeding close together and he knew that these travellers at least had survived another year's journeys. Some of the many geese arriving at the reserve stayed in Lancashire for the whole of the winter. After a few days MOM and a few others took off once more. This time they flew eastwards until they could see the marshes of the north Norfolk coast and the Wash. They flew over the great house at Sandringham. Then they side-slipped down into fields where they knew they would find food and safety until it was time to make their great journey north again.

Glossary

brood *a family of young animals*

calcium *a mineral that is an important part of bones and eggshells*

chick *a baby bird, too young to be able to fly*

corral *an enclosure into which animals are herded*

contour feathers *the feathers that cover the main part of a bird's body—they help to keep the bird waterproof and streamlined*

down *small feathers that lie below the contour feathers, close to the body of most sorts of birds—the down feathers trap air because they are loosely made, so they act like a blanket to keep the birds warm*

flight feathers *the big, stiff feathers on a bird's wings that enable it to fly*

gaggle *a group of geese on the ground*

goslings *young geese*

great circle flight *the route taken by aeroplanes that make long distance flights so that they travel the shortest distance. It is called a great circle because the route follows a line of longitude round the globe—planes going from Europe to North America on a great circle route fly over the North Pole, which is why the migrating geese hear them*

hide *a little hut set up in a place so that people can watch animals without being seen by them, or frightening them*

loch *the Scottish word for a lake*

ornithologist *a person who studies birds*

predators *animals that prey upon other creatures*

preening *the way that birds clean and smooth their feathers with their beaks*

reserve *a place where wildlife is protected*

Reykjavik *the name of the capital city of Iceland*

roost *the place where birds go so that they will be safe to sleep*

scapular feathers *the group of feathers that cover the shoulder area at the top of a bird's wing*

skein *a flock of geese in flight*

stubble *the stalks left in a field once the crop has been harvested*

tundra *the treeless landscape of the Arctic*

Facts about the Pink-footed Goose

➤ **Latin name:** Ansor brachyrhynchus
(An-ser bracky-rin-cuss)
The Latin name means 'the short-beaked goose'.

➤ **Size:** *Head and body length* 60 – 75 cm
Wingspan 135 – 170 cm
The variation is because males are slightly larger
than females.

➤ **Weight:** This changes slightly through the year.

In Britain, *males* weigh about
3 kilograms in October.

In Britain, *females* weigh about
2.5 kilograms in October.

The *young* arriving in Britain after their
first migration weigh slightly less
than their parents.

➤ **World population:** About 250 000

About 200 000 spend their winters in Britain.
Some stay in Scotland, others move south to
Lancashire or Norfolk. Some spend the winter
months in Denmark or other parts of western
Europe. These birds migrate to Spitzbergen to
nest. Most British Pink-footed Geese migrate to
Iceland to nest. A few go to Greenland. In early
June many non-breeding birds fly on from
Iceland to Greenland to moult.

Nest: A mound of grass and other plants collected from the site of the nest. Geese cannot carry things in their beaks, so they cannot make complicated nests. The nest measures 30 – 40 cm across and is about 10 cm high. Inside, the nest is about 22 cm across and 8 cm deep.

Eggs: Most females lay 4 eggs. The eggs are about 78 mm long and 52 mm across at the widest point. They are white but become stained during incubation. Each egg weighs about 132 gm. Only the females sit on (incubate) the eggs. The males stand guard nearby.

Incubation: 26 – 27 days

Chicks:
Chicks are covered with down when they hatch. The can feed themselves but need to be guarded and kept warm by their parents. The chicks get their first feathers and are able to fly when they are about eight weeks old.

Young geese: Young geese stay with their parents through the first winter of their lives and migrate with them the next year. Most Pink-footed Geese breed for the first time when they are three years old.

Lifespan: The greatest age that a Pink-footed Goose is known to have reached is 21 years and five months. This is known because of ringing.

Distances flown in a year:
Pink-footed Geese do not make such long single journeys as some birds, but they travel a great deal in the course of a year. The distance from Scotland to Iceland and back is at least 2200 km.

Flights within Britain:
Geese often fly 10 – 15 km between roosting places and feeding areas, e.g. 20 – 30 km per day for about six months of the year. They may well fly 4000 km each year commuting between food and shelter.

Flights within Iceland:
Flights are fewer and shorter partly because of incubation and partly because the geese are flightless for about three weeks.

During moult:
Parents and chicks may walk long distances finding food. They have been recorded as walking 25 km in a single day.

Index

Arctic fox **20**

arrowhead formation **6, 13**

chicks **21, 22, 23, 24, 27**

Denmark **30**

down **6, 17, 19, 22**

Edinburgh **9**

eggs **8, 17, 19–22, 31**

February **12, 8**

Firth of Forth **8**

flight feathers **24**

Greenland **30**

gosling **23, 26–27**

  see also chicks

gull **20**

hatching **22**

Hebrides **14**

Heckla **21**

hides **10**

Iceland **15–16, 21, 26, 30**

Lancashire **3, 7, 30**

mating **18**

Martin Mere **7, 28**

Midlands **6**

moraines **16**

navigate **14**

nest **16–17, 19–20, 22–23, 30–311**

nets **25–26**

Norfolk **4, 28, 30**

ornithologist **2, 3, 26**

Reykjavik **26**

ring **2–3, 7, 10, 13, 26**

roost **4, 6, 9, 13, 15, 20, 28**

Royal Society for the Protection of Birds **9**

scapular feathers **4**

Scotland **8, 13, 15, 28, 30**

Snowy owl **26**

tundra **21**

Vane Farm **9–10**

Wildfowl and Wetlands Trust **7**